WHAT WE SAW

SIERRA ERNESTO XAVIER

Copyright © 2024 Sierra Ernesto Xavier

ISBN: 978-1-917425-08-7

All rights reserved, including the right to reproduce this book, or portions thereof in any form. No part of this text may be reproduced, transmitted, downloaded, decompiled, reverse engineered, or stored, in any form or introduced into any information storage and retrieval system, in any form or by any means, whether electronic or mechanical without the express written permission of the author.

Also published by Sierra Ernesto Xavier:

Humanity's Rage
The Malady of Love
Distortion

Introduction

In previous publications (*Humanity's Rage*, *The Malady of Love* and *Distortion*), I focused on minimising descriptions of time, place and person, seeking to address thought, emotions and psychology not only via dialogue but also through other aspects of the narration. Of those three texts, *Distortion* was the slight exception, in that the exteriority was described only through dialogue. Like *Distortion*, I sought to minimise the exteriority in this story, *What We Saw*, to what the characters see, and, on occasion, hear.

This is an early piece written before any of my previous publications, and in many ways it is unlike them: there is no dialogue. I wanted to see if a story could move forward without dialogue and also to test the 'to be avoided' second-person narrative. The writing illustrates the evolution of how I managed to use the second person and includes, to a lesser extent, the first and third person too.

One could not describe this story as a fiction of manners or mannerisms, but as a fiction of observational gestures. Here, observations occur through what we see, not just phenomenologically, but also in the interpretation of the inner world. The other is not an object, but a subject with a past, with emotions and feelings. Though the inner world is not verbalised, it is represented and interpreted by the expressions or gestures made by the subject. As we look at the other, we interpret the gaze back at us. We do not know what exactly is going on for the person we are looking at, but we nevertheless interpret something meaningful for us to move on – e.g., are they a friend or foe.

Do we have to be told if someone is frightened or sad or happy? No. We can tell by their body language: glimpses of the psyche. We know this without ever delving into what is frightening them or what is making them sad. Here, the characters understand when they see someone who is lonely or in pain, and thus we do not need to be told the 'what' or the 'why' of their pain. One simply interprets, however accurate that interpretation may be.

I try to use gestures to move the story forward:

> *You glanced at me again but chose not to react, looking away again and electing to habitually sip your drink.*

Without dialogue, there is a focus on the interpretation of what the gestures mean:

> *It was when our eyes met, that moment in time when they were locked together; it was then that I saw the look: the look of a man in desperate loneliness.*

The implication here is that the interpretation provides the motivation. But why would one follow someone in despair or in vulnerability:

> *We understood one another. We were both vulnerable. We knew then that we could satisfy each other's needs.*

The motivation comes not just from the interpretation but also the identification with the self: a mutual interest.

The believability of most texts comes, at least in part, through dialogue where the characters explain to one another their stories, and sometimes from the omniscient narrator, who outlines the 'why'. But here, in *What We Saw*, the reader is given to understand purely from observations and interpretations of the characters without having the situation explained.

I hope the reader will look at *What We Saw* as a different kind of venture from a writer in development.

Sierra Ernesto Xavier

What We Saw

You were sitting at the table when I first saw you. You were alone. You had sensed me looking at you just before you raised your eyes. Perhaps you had seen me before. Perhaps you had seen me turn around. Maybe you then looked down, to avoid my eyes. You need not have bothered. When you looked at me, we knew what we wanted from one another.

You did not say a word. Your look told me everything. It told me that both our needs could be fulfilled.

You sat sitting upright, fastidiously sipping your drink. You glanced at me again but chose not to react, looking away again and electing to habitually sip your drink. It felt as if you had not noticed me, as if I was nothing special. However, that slight pause when you looked at me, the pause that betrayed your formal manner, told me that you had noticed me. It was when our eyes met, that moment in time when they were locked together; it was then that I saw the look: the look of a man in desperate loneliness.

In that moment, before you averted your eyes, you must have seen something in me that you liked. Perhaps it was the way I walked, the way I carried myself that had made me stand out from all the others. Perhaps you liked the confidence in the way I walked over to the bar. Or was it like everyone else when they see someone for the first time: you liked me because of all the superficial elements. You may have liked my smooth, slender legs. You may have liked the shoes that I was wearing – many men like women who wear stilettos. Perhaps, you liked my black suspender belt, or the stockings that they were holding up. Maybe you liked the black see-through knickers that sought to conceal my womanhood, or the black laced basque that I wore. Perhaps it was what was underneath: my body that you were imagining.

Yes, it could have been that: you imagined what was underneath. You saw something about me that you identified with. You had seen a body that in itself was desperate and lonely. A body belied by the confidence of an actress.

You had seen me and I had seen you. We were both uncovered. We understood one another. We were both vulnerable. We knew then that we could satisfy each other's needs.

You continued your pretence of not noticing me. You pretended to ignore my loneliness, to ignore my existence, as if I were not there, as if one could see through me. You seemed to have done this to try to avoid the reflection of your own pain. A pain that had hitherto been solitary.

What We Saw

You continued to sip your drink, observing what was around you. You did that without moving your head. You kept looking forward even as you sipped your drink. Your head stayed still to prevent me from acknowledging your interest in me.

You did not know this, but it was that that had hurt me. It was as if you were reinforcing my desperate solitude. You should have known that. You should have known what it meant to me to be ignored. You should have known from having known your own unhappiness. But in many ways, you were right: those in pain are often the source of pain in others; those in pain find it difficult to acknowledge similar pain in others; your own pain can be re-stimulated by knowing that of others; and you may have to hurt others, by ignoring them, so as not to re-experience your own pain.

You continued not to notice me. Continued to act out your ignorance of me.

You saw me walk towards you. Your head remained still. You did not flinch. You sipped your drink in that formal manner. You did not want my attention. No ... you did not want to attract attention to yourself. You wished that I were not there.

I approached you at your table because I wanted to see what someone else's devastation looked like.

You saw me stand beside the table. You were not looking in my direction, but you saw me. You saw a woman in front of your table, wearing nothing but her lingerie. You did not feel comfortable. I knew you did not feel comfortable. You too were an actor and you were ignoring me. Or at least you were trying to.

I moved to stand in front of you. I moved to stand in your line of sight. I did this so that I could end your pretence. I placed myself in front of you so that you would notice my loneliness; so that you would notice my womanhood, which was trying to hide itself behind the vague semblance of clothing. I wanted you to realize that your loneliness could seek an outlet for its comfort – for you to be consoled. I placed myself in front of you because this confident actress wanted more meaning in her life, wanted to know if her pain could also be resolved.

You betrayed your acting talents by lifting your head to look at me. When you looked into my eyes you saw me look into yours. You had the look of a man who was destitute. And in my eyes, you saw equal poverty – the sort that takes years to build – a lifetime of despair.

You realised you witnessed something that I did not think anyone could see. That was when you lowered your head to avert your gaze.

I sat down at the table just to your left. You maintained your social etiquette by not acknowledging or responding to what you had witnessed: my shame. You continued to look straight ahead and remind yourself of your own secret shame. It became difficult for you, and you turned your head away from me. You did this because you felt I would therefore not see your pain. But then you realized that I had already seen it. That was when you decided to turn your head back towards me to see if I had run away, to see if I felt as disgusted by your desperate loneliness as you did. I had not run away. You saw that I was still sitting there and that I had equal contempt for my own malady.

On seeing my contempt, you turned your head away from me again, this time to look straight ahead. You continued to sip your near empty drink – placing it back on the table. You then heard the clinking of ice in a glass and you turned your head back towards me. You saw me sipping my own drink, looking ahead of me. Then you went back to your acting, you went back to looking forwards and ignoring me.

You closed your eyes for a few moments. It seemed as if you were gathering your thoughts.

You opened your eyes again and reached inside your jacket, into your jacket pocket, and took out an object, which you placed on the table. You kept your hands on the object and slid it towards me. I saw your hands covering the object. I noticed that they were soft and gentle. I noticed they were manicured. That told me that you looked after yourself. That told me that you were sensitive – and that your pain must therefore be doubly tragic. You saw me look up at you. You looked at me. You realized that you had given me a glimpse into your life. You turned to look forward again, taking your hand off the object.

Sierra Ernesto Xavier

I looked down at the envelope on the table. Nothing was written on it. I picked it up and looked inside. There was money in it. I placed the envelope back on the table. You then decided to look at me to see my reaction. You saw me looking forward, sipping my drink. You saw me turn to look at you.

We both knew at that moment that we understood one another. We understood that the relief of our pain was a commodity. We understood that our loneliness could only know moments of reprieve. That these moments had their price. We both knew that. We both knew that our needs could only be fulfilled temporarily; that we no longer had to pretend that they could be satiated; that we could stop acting; that the price of being true to ourselves lay in that envelope.

It seemed strange that the cost of our freedom was based on trading a commodity. It may have seemed like a business transaction – but it was not. Yes, we exchanged goods because we had a common need, but the price of being true to ourselves eliminated the friction from the meeting of two pains – the friction of the greater pain: of whose sorrow might be worse; of who should have more consideration for the other. It is the inequality of the pain – the competition of the greater pain – that destroys the nature and experience of being with one another: it blinds one to the sentiments of the other.

We knew that. We knew that in the envelope lay the significance of our reprieve. With that reprieve in mind, I acknowledged the kind gesture you made.

What We Saw

You mirrored my acknowledgement by nodding your head in agreement.

You saw me stand and pick up the envelope. You saw me standing there waiting for you. You stood up and waited. You did not walk around the table to be by my side. You did not want to hold the hand that I held out for you. Perhaps you were still acting. Perhaps you still wanted to cause me pain. Maybe you wanted to remind me what it was all about – loneliness.

I walked towards the entrance to the rooms at the back of the club. You remained behind me, following, a few steps back, in your formal way. You could see my body from behind. You could see my flesh. See its need for comfort. You saw all this whilst your head remained facing forward – no movement in any direction. Still.

You allowed me to walk through the entrance to the rooms alone. You did not follow me those last few steps. You saw me walk a few yards inside and turn around. I saw your eyes looking at the door frame, tracking it from side to side. You then looked at me. I could see that you did not want to enter: you were not acting; you did not have to say anything, the look in your eyes simply told me.

You gestured with your eyes towards the exit of the club. I knew I could not say no. You were my chance of an 'understanding'. You were my chance of a reprieve with someone who understood; I would have followed you anywhere – the money did not matter.

The money only told us that two lonely people could not have a lifetime together. It told us it was a way of compensating us for that. It created boundaries within which to experience our reprieve. It said that without those boundaries, the two of us would have been doomed to further damage, had we engaged in a bigger ambition.

I followed you to the exit, walking behind you. I could only imagine the loneliness that existed under your clothes.

We picked up our overcoats from the attendant. We put them on. We looked the same: our full-length coats concealing ourselves from the world outside. The coats gave the impression that we were together, that we had been together for some time. That we could be actors again; that we could be partners. We then walked onto our stage by leaving the club.

You led the way, walking ahead of me. Even in our acting you did not want an attachment. You did not want to let the world see something that was not true about yourself. Nor did you want the world to know that we would be using a commodity. It was private. Our loneliness, on both sides, was private. The world would not understand. So I walked those few yards behind you.

It was at one point as we walked that I heard a sound. It was the sound of the sea. It sent a tremor through my body. I had to stop walking. You did not see this, you continued walking.

What We Saw

It was the sea, the voice of the sea, the sounds of the waves. I could hear them. It reminded me ... of death.

Too many people died in the seas. Their putrefied bodies, their decompositions floating in the sea, floating in the waves. I could hear them: it was in the sound of the sea, the crashing of waves. It was in this that they spoke. I could hear the voices as the waves thrust themselves into the shore and then withdrew. They left their suffering behind. You can hear them in seashells. You can hear the sound of the sea.

It was in the water that they had died, and that they remain. They have no gravestones. They are lonely. They are lonely in the water. And the water has kept them. They are like the stillborn: cradled in their amniotic fluid ... alone.

A tremor went through my body; I did not want to be reminded of the sound ... of the dead bodies. I stood still, looking at you walking ahead. The tremor had taken my breath away. I saw you walk ahead, but I could not speak. All I heard was my breath – shallow and barely audible, like the distant sound of the sea.

You somehow knew there was something wrong. You stopped and turned around. You saw me looking at you intently. You had no way of knowing what I was feeling, but somehow you understood. You understood that I could go no further following you. You understood this by the look in my eyes. You understood the look of sadness.

I gestured with my head in a direction to my right, a direction away from the sea. You turned your head back to the direction you were walking. You thought for a moment. You turned your head back towards me. You nodded in agreement.

You saw me turn and walk down the street away from the sea. You followed me. I was leading the way. You walked behind me. You kept the distance between us. You did this because you still did not want anyone to know. You did this because you were out of your comfort zone: you did not know where we were going; you did not like my improvisation. But you knew it had to be tolerated: you knew the reason why we were acting; you knew the reason why we sought a reprieve. The reason lay under our full-length coats.

You kept your dignity – you continued to act. Your head remained forwards as always. You kept me in your sights. You left a space between us because you were afraid that the world would think that we were as one. That if you were too close, people would judge that our transaction was not about being true to ourselves, nor about the moment of reprieve we were seeking. You had the impression that others would believe that you were merely seeking a singular physical pleasure. The world would have been wrong had they thought that.

Our commodity was to free us from the constraints of our limitations. And it was not about one person, but two: two people who wanted to experience a time without self-pity.

What We Saw

You saw me play with you. You saw me play a game. A game in which I would generate echoes in the street by forcing the heels of my stilettos to hammer the ground as I walked. You knew I had done this on purpose. I did not do it to irritate you. I did it to let the world know that a man was following the echoes. That the world could therefore look at you and not me. I did it because it was comforting to let others know that I was a victim, that it was out of necessity that I wanted to confront my despair. You were too far behind for the world to notice that. I was alone in my actions again. I was alone in my disgust. It was then, in that game, that I stopped being an actress. And in not being an actress, I realized that I had left myself exposed to the world. I tried not to create any more echoes. I resumed my pretence.

After a while you saw me stop and turn around. You were some distance away. I saw you stop and look at me. You were not sure what was happening. You thought I could no longer go through with this. That somehow the pain had been stirred in me, that somehow my own anxiety and disgust were preventing me from wanting to be with you. At least, that was what your eyes were telling me. They looked sad. I saw sorrow in your eyes. I almost shed a tear.

You saw me gesture once again with my head, but this time in the direction of the house I stopped outside. You realized that this was the place where we would experience our reprieve. You nodded your head in agreement.

SIERRA ERNESTO XAVIER

You saw me walk to the door of the house. You saw me standing at the door, waiting there for you to follow.

You followed me into the house. It was my house, my place of sadness, my place of loneliness. You could tell that by the fact that my acting was crumbling, that the mask I was wearing was showing signs of anxiety. It was difficult for me to do this, to show you the place where I seemed to be trapped, to show you my place of vulnerability.

You walked past me, maintaining your social etiquette: your head was still facing forwards. You knew how difficult it was for me. I knew you were aware of this because of the empathy I sensed that you had.

I closed the door behind you. You started to look around, but your body remained still. This time your eyes sought a wider vista. You inspected my vulnerability by standing in that one spot, moving your head slowly from one side to the other. You inspected the place thoroughly. Nothing escaped you. You needed to have a look. You needed to familiarise yourself with someone else's vulnerability, someone else's frailty, their sadness. You needed to know this so that you could understand, in our moment of reprieve, what it was that we would both temporarily forget.

You were lost in the obsession that you had, lost in trying to observe my vulnerability, until the point when you saw me looking at you. You then remembered where you were, what you were doing here and what we were trying to achieve.

You turned your head away from me, looking forward again, retreating into your acting. You became aware that you were facing a staircase that led to my private chamber. When you became aware of this, you turned back towards me. You looked at me. It was in that slight pause when our eyes met that I saw the look of a man in confusion, of a man perplexed, in angst. It made me close my eyes.

You saw me with my eyes closed for a few moments. You saw some form of sadness breaking forth from my crumbling mask, saw the change in the colour of my skin. You saw that I was being reminded of the shame and the loneliness. You did not know it was you who had reminded me of it. You just saw me open my eyes and then gesture with my head towards the landing at the top of the staircase.

I turned my head back to you. You then copied my gesture by looking at the top of the staircase. That told me the importance *we* placed on seeking a reprieve.

You saw me walk towards the staircase, climb the first few steps. Your eyes remained in the direction of the stairs. I did not hear you follow me. I stopped on one of the steps. You saw me turn around and look at you. You saw that I was more in need than you. You had seen that my full-length coat had parted. You glimpsed the vague semblance of clothing that was trying to conceal my womanhood.

You saw the desperation of my body. A body in sorrow.

You looked at me. I came back down the staircase and stood in front of you. You saw me offer my hand. You took it. It was the first time we had touched.

You felt the soft palm of my hand. You felt my hand encapsulate yours. I looked at you. You looked at me with some intensity. You closed your eyes for a few moments, forcing them shut. You also closed your mouth firmly, as if you were holding back some form of rage. When you opened your eyes again, I could see a tear about to emerge. You were fighting to keep your suffering hidden from me, preventing it from escaping. You cast your eyes downwards.

I led you up the stairs. I led you to my bedroom, to my private chamber, the place where I am most vulnerable.

You saw me enter the bedroom and followed me. You stood still about a metre into the bedroom. You heard me shut the door behind you as you began to observe the room fastidiously. You continued to scan the room until you saw the bed. This was where your eyes remained focused for some time. You forgot that I was there. It was as if I did not exist for you. You were lonely in your gaze, standing there looking at the place where you would confront your pain and loneliness. Your ignorance of me led me to believe that you might have had second thoughts, that you might not be ready to seek that moment of reprieve.

What We Saw

Perhaps it was that reprieve that was the problem: you could only exist with the pain and loneliness of your life, and without that pain and loneliness, even for a single moment, you might have felt that you had become nothing, that you were lost.

You saw me move in front of the bed. Your head did not move. You did not flinch. You looked at me. You saw a woman standing in front you, in front of the bed, in your line of sight. I stood there so that you could be reminded that this was the place where we both could be consoled.

I took off my coat. It fell to the floor. I was there in front of you wearing nothing but lingerie. You looked at me. You saw my despair. You saw that it existed behind the vague semblance of clothing. It was as if my despair was ashamed to be seen. That it was my femininity and my womanhood that was in despair. You wanted to console this despair.

I approached you. I walked into your comfort zone and stood in front of you. You looked at me. I looked at you. I saw your angst seeking a way out. I saw this in your face. It is as if it was trapped, looking to see where it could escape to.

I bring my hands up to take your coat off. I take your coat off. It falls to the floor.

You then felt my hand in yours. You felt me gently clasp it. I started to move across the bedroom. I led you with my hands. You had no choice but to follow me. We walked to a cupboard. I opened the cupboard door. It revealed a line of lingerie hanging from a rail. You saw that this was not the only time that I had sought a reprieve, that I had tried many times before. But you also realized, having seen my despair, that I had never found it, that I was still destitute.

I ran my hand from one end of the cupboard to the other. You saw my hand move across the sets of lingerie. This may have seemed strange to you – it may have looked like that there were seas of lingerie in front of you.

You selected one set.

You saw me take it and walk to the other side of the room and enter a bathroom. You saw me looking at you as I was about to close the door. I gestured with my head in the direction of the bed. You turned your head towards the bed. You then look back to me. I closed the bathroom door behind me.

You undressed yourself, taking off all your clothes. You freed yourself from your pretence, dismantling the protective shell that had hitherto sustained your life. You stood there naked – vulnerable, exposing your destitution, your suffering, your angst – waiting to be saved from your sorrow. You had taken this risk because you knew that I would be doing the same; that I was not without hurt.

I opened the bathroom door. You saw me in the lingerie that you had chosen. I looked at you. You then saw a look in my eye. You saw a woman almost

What We Saw

in tears, a woman who was shaken to the core, profoundly disturbed by what *she had seen* – your naked body. You saw in my eyes a reaction you had not expected. I had seen that you had seen my reaction.

I took off my lingerie immediately. You saw me do this in a rush. I stood naked in front of you in your line of sight.

You understood why I had rushed. You understood that I needed to show you a mirror image of what I had seen; that my being so perturbed was not about you, but about the recognition of equal sadness, of equal pain, of equal suffering, of the equal poverty we had endured.

You saw me and I saw you. We were both uncovered. We understood one another. We were both vulnerable. We knew we must satisfy the other's needs.

I walked towards you and stood in front of you. It was time to stop acting. We embraced.

*

You lay beside me. Your eyes were shut. I could hear myself breathing. The slow shallowness of my breath: the gentle inhalations ... the gentle exhalations.

It reminded me of the moment of our congress, that moment when I held my breath and my body shuddered with profound emotions. It was also in that moment that the momentum of our congress had reminded me of the sea – the crashing and thrusting of the waves on the shore and their eventual withdrawal. It was at that point that I was reminded of the dead people, of the decompositions floating in and out, who had left their suffering behind. It was a moment of loneliness. The stillborn and putrefied bodies took my breath away.

I could hear the sound of your breath. I could hear the sound of the sea. It was there in your breath also.

We both knew that that moment did not provide the reprieve we needed. It confirmed our desperation – confirmed that neither of us could resolve our pain, that neither of us could escape our loneliness. You were a man destitute, I a woman in despair. We were to be lost at sea like the rest of them, trapped in that existence, carrying the pain wherever we went. We knew that even when we were not acting, when we were being true to ourselves, we were in pain. We knew the moment we had experienced had left its own suffering behind; and that the suffering was the truth.

*

What We Saw

It was through the gentle, shallow sounds of our breathing that we were awakened from our loneliness. The noise we heard disrupted our self-absorption, lifted us out of our shock, out of our post-coital trauma: the realisation that a reprieve was an illusion, that we were by our very nature, by our very being, condemned to loneliness.

It was the rudeness of the noise that interrupted the sound of our waves, that interrupted our meditative breathing: the opening and slamming shut of a car door in anger (an anger no harsher than our destitution). Perhaps it was this, the recognition of a harshness, that lifted us out of our sleep and placed us in a momentary state of needing to seek someone else for a reprieve.

Our eyes were open for a short while: anticipating further disruptions to our trauma; wanting some space so that we could both return to our despair.

There was no rest from the external noise in what we were to experience. There was no space for the reflexive time needed to contemplate our destitution. There were only moments in which we remained focused on that which was external to ourselves.

In those moments we heard the sound of keys in the front door. You turned to me. You did this quickly in a manner that asked me who could this be. You did not say a word. You just gave me an inquisitive look. I could see, in that look of yours, that you wanted this time and space for us alone: that even though we were both solitary, at least we had known someone who could understand. You could not comprehend the idea of someone else violating our place of 'understanding'.

You saw me cast my eyes down and, in my withering mask, a reaction that you had not expected. You saw the colour drain from my face. You saw in me a person who was about to let you down, a person who was 'lost for words', a person who could not look at you for a few moments. You then saw me turn my head away from you to look towards the bedside cabinet. You saw me look at a photograph that you had not noticed before.

You saw me in that photograph. You saw that I was smiling. I was in my wedding dress. You saw that I was smiling and holding the arm of my husband beside me.

I turned my head to look at you. You looked at me. As we looked at one another we heard the front door open and close. It was in that moment, when our eyes locked together, that I could see the hurt I had caused. I hoped that you could see the 'sorry' in mine.

You got out of bed and began to dress. You did this in your efficient manner. It seemed that you were leaving in some kind of desperation: a desperation that you did not deserve; a desperation whereby I had reinforced some of your pain; the pain of a man who, in his attempt to seek a reprieve, has had hurt inflicted upon him.

What We Saw

You continued to dress in haste. We heard footsteps on the stairs. You saw me get out of bed and walk around to you. Then I quickly walked to the window beside the wardrobe that faced the bathroom. You saw me open the window. We heard the footsteps getting louder. As I looked at you, you saw a form of desperation in my eyes. You also saw that I was about to gesture a final, undignified act. I had seen in your face a capitulation to a form of despondency. A despondency greater than that which I had seen in you before – a capitulation into helplessness.

I gesture with my head in the direction of the open window.

You turned your head to look at the bedroom door as you heard the footsteps approaching the top of the stairs. You seemed to have paused for something. You looked like you were thinking. You turned your head back towards the window and then to me. You saw in my body something that you had not hitherto seen: the abjection of my poverty. You then looked into my eyes and saw that I was truly trapped in my place of vulnerability. That my sorrow was more profound because I was lonely, destitute and in despair inside a marriage. That even though I would still have been destitute had I not been married, I inflicted this pain on myself because I had chosen to remain inside the marriage. You had seen that I was harming myself. You also saw that I could not fully understand nor see that for myself.

You moved towards the window and exited.

The bedroom door handle began to turn.

I returned to the bed.

He entered the room. He saw me in bed. He saw that the window was open. He walked towards the bed and looked at me. My eyes were closed. He leant over and kissed me on my forehead.

He stood up again, took off his necktie and walked around the bed. He started to walk towards the bathroom. He had seen my lingerie on the floor. He then looked at me as I lay in bed pretending to be asleep. He paused and remained still for a few moments.

He continued to walk towards the bathroom, taking a few steps more. But when he saw a used sheath on the floor he stopped and looked at me again. He looked at me lying in bed pretending to be asleep. My eyes still closed. Then he turned his head to looked at the used sheath again and then continued to walk towards to the bathroom.

It was in the bathroom that he again surveyed my clothes: my stilettos, my stockings, my suspender belt, my knickers, my basque. The vague semblance of clothing on the floor. He noticed something underneath: an envelope, with money protruding. It was as if the pile of scant clothes was trying to hide it, to conceal the truth - trying to cover the pain.

He walked out of the bathroom and towards the bedroom door with a sense of purpose. He opened the bedroom door, left, and closed the door behind him.

I opened my eyes and looked around the room. I heard his footsteps fading down the staircase. I got out of bed. I made a pretence of waking up, of having heard the bedroom door shut, of having waited most of the night for my husband to arrive, of having waited in bed ready for us to consume the night. I started acting again.

I saw the lingerie on the floor; the mantle that protects my suffering. I dressed myself so that my despair could hide behind some form of clothing, so that my shame did not need to be entirely exposed. I knew that my need to be consoled could never be requited. I knew that the moments I so longed for were an awakening to my existence – that I would have to sustain myself as an actress. And in being an actress I would have to tell him that I waited for him, that I wanted him to see me in my beauty, that the thought of him made me feel that a need for a prelude or overture was unnecessary for us to consummate the night and that I dressed myself out of concern that he had left the room.

I heard his footsteps again. This time they were louder. I had heard him climbing the staircase.

I felt something cold under my feet as I dressed myself in my lingerie. I looked down. I saw the used sheath. The bedroom door handle began to turn. I kicked the sheath under the bed.

He entered the bedroom. He saw me standing there waiting for him. He shut the bedroom door; his hands were behind him on the door handle, so that he could lean back against the door as it closed. He looked at me and smiled. I smiled. He tells me that tonight will be the night of our passion, of our honesty; that we are to be as one in congress; that we are to be together in our moments of reprieve; that these moments can only occur, can only have significance, inside a marital union.

I saw that he was hurt. I heard his pain: he never talked about honesty or togetherness. He wanted to express his anguish through the union of our intimacy.

I looked at him. He was smiling. I kept smiling too. I started to undress myself again. This time I undressed myself in a manner designed to effect a response. He could neither see my poverty nor my suffering. He could only see my acting, which was how I wanted it.

A naked body awaited him. He looked at my body and admired it for a while.

I saw him walk towards me. I saw him standing in front of me – looking at me, still smiling. It was the moment we were to console one another. It was the moment that I was to console him, the moment of our lie.

He leant forward to kiss me. I leant forward to meet him. I tried to embrace him while our lips were together. He moved his arm from behind him. It broke my embrace. He lifted his arm above his head. I parted from his lips. I looked at his hand. I saw a kitchen knife in his fist. I looked at him.

In that moment, that slight pause when our eyes met, the moment in time when our eyes were locked together, it was then that I whispered in a shallow breathe ... his name.

*

As I lay on the floor, my eyes were shut. I could hear myself breathing: the gentle inhalations ... the gentle exhalations ... slowly fading ... slowly dying.

The thrust of the knife had taken my breath away. It was in that moment that my body shuddered with profound emotions. It was also a moment, in the momentum of the knife, which reminded me of the sea – the sharp thrusts of the waves and their eventual withdrawal. I was soon to be with the dead people, leaving my suffering behind.

Author's Note

The emphasis on what the characters saw develops lethargically, one might say. (I see your pain; I have pain; our pain is reflected in one another; we understand what we want; our needs can be met ...) Our story is a slow build, as you would expect of one that is driven forward by gestures – each gesture is significant, each has a meaning. As an observational piece, it is conveyed from an individual's interpretation of one gesture at a time: what it is for you; what you may have seen in me; what I understand to be the bridge that forms our connection.

I sought not to explain the characters' loneliness or despair or angst, past or present, but merely intended to say that the lives of the two main characters contain these experiences and only they know what they are, only they recognise these experiences. The story is therefore like a puppet show that one watches: no need to be over-involved, nor to be taken away by the story – just to observe, as the characters within the story do.

www.ingramcontent.com/pod-product-compliance
Lightning Source LLC
Chambersburg PA
CBHW070341120526
44590CB00017B/2973